D1706590

Simple
Brian Holland

Cover Image and Design: Amanda Redd

First printing 2023

This is dedicated to my amazing wife, Kelley. I've never met anyone who so faithfully and joyfully serves Jesus like you do. Simple obedience all because you love Jesus. I love you!

table of contents.

introduction.   4

chapter 01. not just another day.   11

chapter 02. help.   24

chapter 03. it can't be that simple.   36

chapter 04. even when it makes no sense.   48

chapter 05. do it.   65

chapter 06. the importance of firsts.   77

chapter 07. unexpected results.   89

introduction.

Let this sink in. As I write these words, there are about eight billion people on planet earth. Trying to understand such a large number makes it easy to see yourself as "just one" of those eight billion. But then on top of that humbling thought, if you call yourself a follower of Jesus, he calls you to reach all of them with the love of Jesus. Do you feel overwhelmed just yet? Hold on. Let's add on a couple more things. There are some thirty million people who are slaves in the world today. Every three seconds, a child dies somewhere in the world because he or she will not have enough food to eat. The task seems too big. The call seems overwhelming and unreachable. And you? Me? We are just one person out of eight billion.

It's so easy to feel insignificant and unimpressive, isn't it? You are just one and you have your own issues, baggage, and insecurities that you are trying to work through. You are trying to keep up with the pace of life, shuttling kids from soccer to youth group, or from dance to karate lessons, or you are the kid being shuttled. Or maybe you are trying to survive financially while keeping your marriage intact. Or you are a student overwhelmed with school while having to make decisions that will impact you for the rest of your life. Perhaps you are retired, getting to enjoy some downtime while still longing to live out the purpose you've always sensed that you've had. Or maybe you feel lost and out of control as the addiction that you have tried so hard to break keeps backing you into a corner, making you feel hopeless and defeated. Or maybe you are almost ready to, or have just started this journey with Jesus, wondering exactly where you fit in and what you are supposed to do. But what can you do that will be of any true impact when you think about everything going on in our world? What can I do?

The answer? You can dent eternity. How? By doing this one thing: fill jars. Of course, this may not make sense three paragraphs in, but it will later on. Just remember that the key to seeing Jesus do the miraculous is not to create the miraculous but to be obedient in the mundane, because faithfulness in the mundane is what ushers in the miraculous work of Jesus.

The second chapter of John's gospel reveals the account of Jesus performing his very first miracle. What did he do? He turned water into wine. He was attending a wedding celebration with his mom, his siblings, and his disciples. In that day, a wedding celebration would have lasted anywhere from a few days to over a week. While there, the problem shows itself: the hosts do not have enough wine for the guests. So, Jesus turns water into wine. Of course, there is more to this passage than that one "simple" fact, but that is the problem that showed up unannounced.

For those of you who have been brought up in the church, you have probably at least heard this passage read. You have possibly heard this story told. *Water into wine*. But please do not tune out (especially since this is still the introduction of the book). You may be reading this, completely in love with Christ and still in awe of, or at least somewhat impressed by, this first miracle that quietly launched his earthly ministry. Or you may be the person who has heard so many sermons and stories about this passage of Scripture that you have closed yourself off to ever learning anything new from it. And what about those of you who grew up "in the church" and, because of your experience, are turned off by anything resembling Christianity? Or maybe you have never even heard this passage of Scripture because you don't believe in God, let alone read the book that Christians believe God wrote.

Wherever you are in this adventure of life so far, welcome to the journey that will (at least I pray that it will) free you from a man-made, religion-driven, cheap-miracle-creating culture of Christianity, the one mixed with an American culture of immediate gratification, neglecting our call to be still and know God. A culture that expects God to work according to the schedules that we keep on our smartphones rather than according to the perfect purpose and timetable of his will. A culture that has begun to bow down to the "elephant" or the "donkey" of American politics instead of laying prostrate before the Lamb of God. I'm convinced that it is time to say goodbye to overworked and ineffective lives and ministries and get back into the true call that Christ invites us into: the miraculous mundane.

It is in this place of the miraculous mundane that every person understands, accepts, and delights in the truth that he or she plays a part in the supernatural story of God's continuous intervention. It is in this place of the miraculous mundane where your obedience to the simple instructions of Jesus is the thing that brings about the most effective and joyful results. It is in this place of the miraculous mundane that you are confronted with the motivation of why you live your life the way that you do. It is in this place of the miraculous mundane that you learn to stop merely living for Christ and learn to live by and with him.[1] As Ralph Waldo Emerson is quoted as saying, "...the invariable mark of wisdom is to see the miraculous in the common."

We want the front-row seats so that we can see Jesus do the unexplainable. We want the birds-eye view to see Jesus do the miraculous in and around us. We even want to be part of the process, being able to tell the stories to the following generations about that one time when Jesus did that one thing. We want it, but what are we willing to do to see it?

"I would die for Christ."

"I would go to the ends of the earth for Jesus."

"I would be the most sold-out follower of Jesus, going into the most dangerous places."

We must remember that Jesus' call is not to something safe. There are stories in Scripture where people are arrested and beaten for their faith. Keep in mind, there is more persecution of Christians going on in the world today than ever before. Friends, he is calling us to faithfully live out *his will*, trusting him with whatever dangers he wants us to

---

[1] John 15:4-5

face wherever he decides for us to go? In other words: we accept his call to follow him no matter what and no matter where, even if his will leads us to the unnoticed ministry path. The first step is to follow him, and for some this simply means going across the street with the gospel before getting on a plane to go across the world. Why? Because our mission field starts in our zip codes.

And please understand as we move through these chapters, much of the conversation that is presented as happening between Jesus and other characters are from a place of creative license unless it is clearly stated in the passage. But what if? What if it happened this way? I have no desire to re-write Scripture but rather to take us into the story of it by trying to bridge the gap between then and now while never taking away from the original meaning and message of God's word.

So, again, the invitation is simply to follow Jesus. And from there, in all humility, to bow in reverent adoration in honor of Jesus as we simply do whatever he says. As the Methodist Covenant Prayer reads:

> "I am no longer my own, but Thine. Put me to
> what Thou wilt, rank me with whom Thou wilt;
> put me to doing, put me to suffering; let me be

employed for Thee or laid aside for Thee, exalted for Thee or brought low for thee; let me be full, let me be empty; let me have all things, let me have nothing; I freely and heartily yield all things to Thy pleasure and disposal. And now, O glorious and blessed God, Father, Son, and Holy Spirit, Thou art mine, and I am Thine. So be it. And the covenant, which I have made on earth, let it be ratified in heaven. Amen."

No matter where he takes us or what he calls us to do, we are called to be faithful, even in the mundane. Charles Spurgeon once said, "The repetition of small efforts will accomplish more than the occasional use of great talents." We don't see the small efforts as being all that effective or impressive, but I truly believe that we would be amazed if we looked back over time and saw all of the small efforts that truly changed history. So, let's spend some time together dreaming up ways to see how we can continue changing history, one small and mundane step at a time, all because we did one thing: we filled some jars.

chapter 01. not just another day.

"On the third day there was a wedding at Cana in Galilee, and the mother of Jesus was there. Jesus also was invited to the wedding with his disciples." — John 2:1-2

On his way to Cana for a wedding, Jesus met Andrew, Simon, James, John, Philip and Nathanael, some of his soon-to-be disciples. These men were not looking to be found. They weren't looking to become famous, forever known as a member of "The Twelve" in the #1 best-selling book of all time. They weren't waiting to be found as a disciple. The fact that they were working a trade meant that they did not make the cut to be apprenticed to a Rabbi, so that dream of being a disciple was long gone. They were not of the religious and pious pedigree that could be part of the religious leadership.

But these guys met THE Rabbi of all rabbis who saw something different in them. Even though these men came from different places and backgrounds, there was something unifying about this carpenter from the tiny village of Nazareth.

Andrew was a disciple of John the Baptist who heard John's proclamation about Jesus being "The Lamb of God!" This made Andrew so intrigued that he began to follow Jesus from a distance. But Jesus knew he was being followed. So, when Andrew was close enough, Jesus turned around and asked him this question, "What are you seeking?".[2] The meaning behind this question seems to go beyond the casual, "What's going on, bro? Can I help you with something?" It was as if Jesus was going after the motivation of Andrew's life, as if he was asking a question full of so much meaning that Andrew had no answer to give to him. He did not know what to say except to ask Jesus where he was staying. And all that Jesus had to say was, "Come and you will see."[3] Andrew had no idea what following Jesus meant. He had no clue the adventure that he had just committed himself to. He simply accepted Jesus' hospitable invitation to spend the rest of the day with him. And that one decision changed the course of his whole life.

Andrew spent the rest of the day with Jesus. I wonder if that single question played helplessly on repeat in Andrew's mind. "What are you seeking?" As he tried to

---

[2] John 1:38

[3] John 1:39

answer maybe Andrew realized that it was the question of a lifetime—not merely a question posed to him that afternoon for that afternoon. The conversation with himself probably went on and on, all the while leaving Andrew speechless and his mind spinning simply because of the time he spent with Jesus.

After his first encounter with Jesus, Andrew had to find his brother, Simon. This was Andrew's priority and only mission. You see, Andrew had already come to his own conclusion about the identity of Joseph and Mary's boy. "We have found the Messiah."[4]   Jesus did not perform any miracles while they were together that day, yet his conversation with the carpenter-turned-Rabbi from Nazareth still came to that divinely inspired conclusion. Jesus was the Messiah. And the first thing that Andrew had to do was find his brother and tell him the good news. Andrew searched and looked for his brother, and when Andrew found him, Simon went with him to meet Jesus.

Jesus' first words to Simon were, "So you are Simon the son of John? You shall be called Cephas."[5] Peter. Rock. Really? Did Jesus know who he was talking to or talking

---

[4] John 1:41

[5] John 1:42

about? Absolutely. However, Jesus also knew who he would later become. He had it all planned and worked out already.

Philip was next. However with Philip, Jesus approached him with this simple invitation, "Follow me." It was simple in the fact that it was only two words in length, but it was life-changing in impact. Philip accepted the invitation, but first he went to find Nathanael to tell him the amazing news. "We have found him of whom Moses in the Law and also the prophets wrote, Jesus of Nazareth, the son of Joseph."[6] Philip was tell Nathanael that the Messiah whom they had been waiting for was Jesus, to which Nathanael sarcastically asked, "Can anything good come out of Nazareth?"[7] Of course, Jesus "impressed" Nathanael in such a way that by the end of the conversation he said to Jesus, "Rabbi, you are the Son of God! You are the King of Israel!"[8] Nathanael was in. He could not turn back now because he had come face-to-face with the Son of God.

These disciples were simply living their lives. They were having an ordinary day until Jesus stepped in and invited them to something that would completely "mess"

---

[6] John 1:45

[7] John 1:46

[8] John 1:49

everything up. His simple invitation of "follow me" was a bidding to walk more intimately with God-incarnate than any other person up to that point had ever experienced. They would have the front-row seat to the miraculous—every day. But this adventure began because Jesus showed up on an ordinary day. It happened during the mundane of their lives. It started when they least expected it. Let's face it: God doesn't work according to our preconceived ideas. God, in his holiness, does what he wants, when he wants, based on how he wants things to be, according to his will, to receive glory. And he never really asks us if we approve.

And now back to the wedding. Whose wedding was it? We have no idea. Their names are never mentioned. The family is never talked about. All we know is that Mary and Jesus were both invited. His disciples? We have no clue. I picture them being the ultimate wedding crashers. But why would the family invite Jesus? Well let's think about it. Who usually gets invited to a wedding? In my humble opinion, people you like and people you love - the ones that you actually want to be there. And I know that I'm looking at this from my 21st-century perspective, but this causes me to believe that Jesus was likable. This couple and family wanted Jesus to be there. This is obvious because he received an invitation to the big day. And he showed up. And I bet he was a blast.

For too long Jesus has been portrayed by so many as boring and serious. Think about how you pictured Jesus when you were growing up if you pictured him at all. If you are anything like me, you never saw him as someone with emotions. He never got mad, or sad, or glad. He was, for some reason, the most mild-mannered man to ever walk on planet earth. He would never upset anyone or cause any type of disruption. He was the Mr. Rogers of the first century. And the only problem with this portrayal of Christ is the Bible. If Jesus were a boring man who never had any type of emotional change or response, but rather remained constantly mediocre, why would people ever want to crucify that type of guy? The same way that no one could ever think about crucifying Mr. Rogers, so no one could think of crucifying the fake Jesus that we have created in our minds.

Jesus was the type of person who would weep over Jerusalem as he rode into the city the week before his death. He was the type of person who went off one day at the temple. As he looked around the temple and saw it turned into a market of thieves instead of a house where people could come and pray, he had enough collected rage that he actually made a make-shift whip and went after the money-changers, turning over their tables and letting their "acceptable sacrifices" run free. He wept over the death of his friend Lazarus, even though he knew he would raise him back to life.

By looking at Jesus through the lenses of the gospels, Jesus is the epitome of character and personality. There were times when he was with the crowds, ministering to as many people as possible. There were times when he would leave the crowds so that he could get alone and be with his heavenly Father. He would preach to the thousands from a boat, and he would meet with Nicodemus late at night for a one-on-one question and answer session. There was a time when he started a conversation with a Samaritan woman with questionable character by a well at mid-day, and a time when he rescued a woman from being stoned to death because she was caught in the act of adultery. He was an incredible and captivating teacher. He was a compassionate and understanding friend. He was able and gracious as a healer. He was patient but challenging as a Rabbi. And I'm convinced that he was fun.

He was liked and likable. He was gracious and loving. He was rugged and strong. His hands were calloused and worn from all the carpentry that he did, but tender enough to hold a child on his lap while he spoke about the kingdom of God. He defended the oppressed and celebrated over the liberated. He forgave his accusers and paid the penalty for the sin of the world. But I just cannot imagine Jesus not having a sense of humor (remember that log in your own eye teaching? With the perfect object lesson, that teaching is hilarious). Throughout the gospels we see the character qualities of Jesus revealed. Why would he leave joy and humor out of his character and personality when the fruit of knowing Christ is joy in the Holy Spirit?

So, what would he be doing at a wedding?

The truth of the matter is that the passage never tells us exactly what Jesus was doing while at the wedding. All that it tells us is that he was invited and that he obviously showed up. Since that is it, I'm thinking that maybe we are supposed to walk away seeing him in our minds at that wedding doing what everyone else would be doing at that wedding. Celebrating.

He was not "performing any miracles" since what he did at this wedding was his first one. Rather, he was the carpenter's boy, invited to a wedding. He was "just Jesus" to everyone there. And even though there was something extraordinary about this "normal" carpenter, here he was at a friend's wedding on an ordinary day. He was a guest but not necessarily the guest of honor. And for Jesus, he was okay with this since he understood that he did not seem any more impressive than anyone else there. Plus, the couple were the guests of honor that day, and Jesus celebrated them as he quietly watched with joy-filled reserve.

You see, on a prior ordinary day, this "ordinary" carpenter approached some fishermen (while they were mending their nets) and invited them to drop everything and follow him. An ordinary day with mundane tasks and responsibilities turned into an encounter with the one who would change their lives forever, all of which happened at a wedding.

And that is still what happens today. Jesus is still "on the hunt." On days when school projects are due, bills need to be paid, where dinners need to be made, kids need to be bathed, lawns need to be mowed, dogs need to be fed, trash needs to be emptied, friends get sick and family members die, there is a personal God who is calling to you with the very same invitation that he gave to those very first disciples two-thousand years ago. "Follow me."

The problem is that the noise of our days can so easily

drown out the still and soft whisper of the Holy Spirit calling us to Jesus. The important has been replaced by the immediate when prioritizing our lives, and rather than reevaluate this, we want him to shout over the din. We read passages in the Bible when God showed up to Moses in a burning bush, wondering why God will not show up to us in that same way. Isaiah had this amazing encounter with God when he saw the Lord on his throne. [8] It only seems right and fair that we should have that same encounter with Jesus. Peter, James, and John, later in their journey with their Rabbi, encountered the transfigured and glorified Jesus on that cold evening that left them terrified, in awe, and speechless.

But us? "Raise your hand if you want to accept Jesus into your life." And we do that with every head bowed and every eye shut, anonymous and camouflaged hoping that what we just did really did something, all the while not quite sure. We do not understand that Jesus met and called his disciples on mundane and ordinary days while they were doing mundane and ordinary tasks. We walk through our days just wishing for one of those "Bible-sized" encounters with the living God, all the while missing him every single day because we are not willing to see him meeting us in the ordinary, calling us into something that is extraordinary. We are neglecting and ignoring the very presence of God inside of us through the Holy Spirit, which is so much more impressive than a burning bush that Moses was allowed to see.

Then again why would he call us? We are nothing special. We know where we fail. We know where we fall short. Our insecurities, the good things that we intend to do, only to fall short in making them happen. We know the motivations of our hearts and how so very often we are serving ourselves while we pretend that we are helping others. We know our own doubts. We know the pain that we have gone through and the addictions that we have, even if no one else knows. We know us. Why would he want us?

Maybe this will answer that question for you:

Fear not, for I have redeemed you;

I have called you by name, you are mine.

When you pass through the waters, I will be with you;

and through the rivers, they shall not overwhelm you;

When you walk through fire you shall not be burned,

and the flame shall not consume you.

For I am the LORD your God,

the Holy One of Israel, your Savior...

because you are precious in my eyes,

And honored, and I love you,...[9]

Late one night I was sitting on the carpet of my boy's bedroom at 12:30am as I read that passage. I was going through a time of doubt and self-condemnation where I heard in my mind how bad I was at being a follower of Jesus, husband, dad, pastor,... and the list just kept going on and on. I could not sleep. So, for some strange reason, I went into their room to read my Bible on my phone. I came across Isaiah 43, read the verses above, and wept quietly as I laid on my stomach with my face in the carpet, overcome by what God was speaking over me. After about 10 minutes, I sat up and looked at my boys. I still didn't understand why I was in there, but then this question came to my mind, "Why do you love these boys?" I responded, "Because I'm their dad." And then I heard by faith, "And that's why I love you." And then I knew it was God speaking to me as only a loving father can. And those few words, for he does not need to say much, changed everything. I went back to bed and slept well, knowing that I was loved and adored by my Father in heaven.

Even in our shortcomings God loves the ordinary us.

---

[9] Isaiah 43:1b-3a, 4a

When we struggle seeing the pieces of who we are that would cause God to want us, we need to listen for his whisper: "I've always loved the ordinary." He even became ordinary so that he could have the ordinary us.

So, the next time you're at a wedding and attend the reception, stop and picture Jesus there with you. There is no way it will be just another day. And get ready. He is about to get the party started.

chapter 02. help.

"When the wine ran out, the mother of Jesus said to him, 'They have no wine.' And Jesus said to her, 'Woman, what does this have to do with me? My hour has not yet come.'" — John 2:3-4

"Oops" and "Uh-oh." These two little phrases can bring a completely different feeling based on who is saying them. When a little boy is coloring and the marker that he is using runs out of ink, he may say "uh oh" and the problem can be fixed immediately. When a little girl can't find her other shoe, the same thing is true. It can be fixed without much effort.

However, if you are getting your haircut and the stylist says, "uh oh," all of the fear within your soul comes out in chills all over your body. If you are having surgery and the doctor says, "oops," be especially thankful that you were under anesthesia and didn't know about the mistake made.

What do you do when the "uh-ohs" happen? Where do you turn? In this passage, the "uh oh" that happened was a much bigger deal than it seems to us today. The problem? They ran out of wine. That's right. The beverage of choice at this celebration had run out. That would have been fine if the wedding was finishing up, but nowhere in the text does it show that the celebration was closing any time soon. Jewish weddings, during the first century, were not one-day events. William Barclay explains:

> "The wedding festivities lasted far more than one day. The wedding ceremony itself took place late in the evening, after a feast. After the ceremony, the young couple were conducted to their new home. By that time it was dark and they were conducted through the village streets by the light of flaming torches and with a canopy over their heads. They were taken by as long a route as possible so that as many people as possible would have the opportunity to wish them well. But a newly married couple did not go away for their honeymoon; they stayed at home; and for a week they kept open house. They wore crowns and dressed in their bridal robes. They were treated like a king and queen, were actually addressed as king and queen, and their word was law. In a life where there was much poverty and constant hard work, this week of festivity and joy was one of the

supreme occasions."[10]

"But what's the big deal?" It is so easy to look at this problem through the lenses of the 21st century which has a BevMo or grocery store to save the day. There was no such solution for this problem. For the wedding hosts to run out of wine was a major shame for the family. It showed everyone in attendance that the hosts were unable to provide for everyone invited to the wedding. This would have been a horribly embarrassing situation and an awkward way for this young couple to begin their life together. As William Barclay once again points out, "At any time, the failure of provisions would have been a problem, for hospitality in the middle east is a sacred duty; but for the provisions to fail at a wedding would be a terrible humiliation for the bride and the bridegroom."[11]

Either the chatter between family members was overheard by Mary, or even quite possibly, the family came to Mary with the problem looking for any ideas for a solution. Some have even claimed that Mary was the one in charge of

---

[10] Barclay, William, "The Gospel of John, Volume 1"; The Westminster Press, Philadelphia, pg. 96-97.
[11] Ibid, pg. 97.

the needs for the wedding, kind of like being the wedding coordinator today. In any case the problem was brought to her attention. Her first thought, at least how I picture it in my mind, was "uh oh." She had to help solve this problem. So, she went to her oldest boy. She walked up to Jesus and said, "They have no more wine." With all the chatter and celebrating going on I can picture Jesus having to lean in to hear what his mom just told him. As it registered, he was perplexed. Why? He was a carpenter. He was a man who was making a living by creating furniture out of wood, not by making wine out of grapes. Unless Jesus had his own side moonshine business that Scripture did not mention, it seems random that Mary would go to Jesus with this problem.

Now I know that some of you reading this will think, "Of course she would go to Jesus. He is the one who can do the miraculous." And I agree with you that he can. However, up to this point, he had not revealed his glory through performing the miraculous. He was "just Jesus." Why would she go to Jesus with this problem? A problem that seemed to be something that he had no expertise in or ability to fix? And maybe Jesus was wondering the same thing because he answered her by saying, "Woman, what does this have to do with me? My hour has not yet come."

Maybe the life-changing experience that she went through as a new mom some thirty years before was the catalyst for her decision to go to Jesus with this issue. To hear from the angel Gabriel that she was pregnant while a virgin, that the baby that she was carrying was the coming Messiah, the Son of God (what so many other young moms prayed they would get to experience), was a pretty miraculous birth announcement for a teenage girl to receive. When she asked, "How will this be, since I am a virgin?", the angel responded to her saying, "The Holy Spirit will come upon you, and the power of the Most High will overshadow you; therefore the child to be born will be called holy—the Son of God. And behold, your relative Elizabeth in her old age has also conceived a son, and this is the sixth month with her who was called barren. **For nothing will be impossible with God"**.[12]

To Mary, the problem was real, but the solution was close at hand. She was told 30 years before that her son would change things. It just seemed natural for her to go to the one whose birth was announced by angels. People may not have known who Jesus was, but Mary had been told of his identity from the very beginning. "Nothing will be

---

[12] Luke 1:35-37, ESV (**emphasis** added)

impossible with God." In this light it seems completely natural for her to go to Jesus. And it should be completely natural for us to go to Jesus as well.

Have you ever noticed how difficult it is for us to admit that we actually have a problem? It seems to be ingrained into all of us that we are to be self-sufficient, that we should be able to handle anything and everything that comes our way. To ask for help is a sign of weakness, and weakness displayed is not an option. So, because of our pride, we keep it to ourselves. We forget about God's invitation to come to him with everything, casting all our anxieties on him because he truly does care for us. We forget that Jesus is the one who said that apart from him we can do nothing. We give up our intimate relationship with the Holy Spirit because of our pride, only to see the result be failure and lack of intimacy with our Creator.

Or maybe, we just don't really believe that Jesus can or will actually do anything to fix it. How often have you prayed and not seen the miraculous happen in the same way that it happened in the Bible? So many of us have faced difficult situations and not seen God "save the day" like he did "back in the day." We automatically jump to believe that Jesus must not care about us when we don't see him work in the immediate. For example, in Mark 5 Jesus healed the woman with the flow of blood. This condition would have made the woman unclean in her society. When she saw Jesus, she believed that if she could just touch the hem of his garment that she would be healed. So, she went for it. She made her way through the crowd, pushing her way forward as a woman with nothing to lose and everything to gain, and touched the hem of his garment and was immediately healed.

Just like that: she was healed. Immediately. But we forget that she had struggled with this for 12 years. Because we read it in Scripture, it is easy for us to ignore how long she struggled because we are so overcome by the immediate. But those 12 years of her life, and having to face the struggles spiritually, emotionally, and physically that came with it, brought her to a place of meeting her Savior and being touched by Jesus. Her struggles brought about her ability to witness and experience firsthand the reality of the miraculous. I have often wondered if that woman would have given up the experience of being personally healed by Jesus for 12 years of pain-free living. Would you? Would I?

"But Brian, I know Jesus. I have gone to him and nothing has changed. I have cried out to him and I'm still facing the same thing." And to this I can say that I completely understand where you are coming from. I have been there. I will be there again. But just like Jesus had a greater purpose in the suffering than this woman's experience and had a purpose in the timing behind when he would heal her, so too he is doing something to prepare you for what he is going to do *through* you.

The truth of the matter is that Jesus may not always work in the "immediate," but he is always at work. And his timing is perfect. In the middle of the pain, it never feels this way. But, if you are anything like me, you can look over the years of your life, so far, and see how God has stepped in and done incredible things at just the right time. Any time God steps in is the miraculous.

So, let me encourage you by reminding you that you can't do it. You can't do it alone, and Jesus knows it.

Does that help at all? You cannot do it alone. You will feel overwhelmed as a student, wondering how you're going to get everything done. You will feel overwhelmed as a parent, wondering if you are doing anything right in raising your kids. You will feel like you are not being a good enough Christian, failing God more than feeling like you are making him proud. The expectations of others around you will build and become too much for you to handle. In ministry you will wonder if it is all worth it because you are not even sure if you're making a difference. And Jesus knows it. And if Jesus already knows it, then we need to drop the pride and go to the one who can handle it.

It is expected by God that we would ask him for help — constantly. We have somehow missed this. We are so focused on living for Christ, living our lives in such a way as to bring him praise, glory and honor so that he would be proud of us. But the problem with living for Christ is that most of the time we are not inviting Christ to walk with us. Rather we invite him to sit back and watch what we can accomplish for him, without any help from him.

The problem with that mentality is that it is absolutely and completely impossible. Jesus knows that we will fail more than we think that we will. Self-reliance is not a sign of strength but of pride. Taking responsibility for one's self and what God has entrusted to and asked of a person to manage is one thing, but to live a life of pride-driven self-reliance is not a mark of strong, honorable character, but rather of sin-entangled pride that only leads to arrogance instead of a spirit of humility. Jesus is the one who poetically said, "I am the vine; you are the branches. Whoever abides in me and I in him, he it is that bears much fruit, for apart from me you can do nothing."[13]

So that means that Jesus is not wanting us to live for him apart from a reliance upon him, but rather abide in him and live this life for him by him. And that is why he gave us his Holy Spirit as "The Helper." It is the job of the beloved Holy Spirit of God to help us as we strive to live the life that Christ paid for us to live--not independent of him, trying to prove to him how strong and capable we are on our own, but rather completely dependent upon him, showing him how much we have grown in our relationship with Jesus as we have relied upon him. Growing in Christ reveals our utter dependence upon Christ.

So, ask for help. Jesus gave us his Holy Spirit to help us now and every day, and then gave us this truth to point us back to Jesus in everything. The writer of Hebrews says it this way, "Since then we have a great high priest who has passed through the heavens, Jesus, the Son of God, let us hold fast our confession. For we do not have a high priest who is unable to sympathize with our weaknesses, but one who in every respect has been tempted as we are, yet without sin.

---

[13] John 15:5, ESV

Let us then with confidence draw near to the throne of grace, that we may receive mercy and find grace to help in time of need."[14]

The door is always open. We are invited to confidently draw near to Jesus, the author and perfecter of our faith, any time that we want with anything that we have, and he will help us. And not just help, but compassionate and sympathetic help with power that brings about his desired results and outcome. Why compassion and sympathetic help? Because he completely understands what it is like to be human. He knows the pain and trials. He understands temptation far more than we ever will, and yet he never gave in to it. He has experienced the limitations that we have experienced and yet still accomplished the impossible. The writer of Psalm 103 says it this way, "As a father shows compassion to his children, so the LORD shows compassion to those who fear him. For he knows our frame; he remembers that we are dust."[15] He understands. He has compassion. He has the solution.

We must ask for God's help to make it a natural

---

[14] Hebrews 4:14-16, ESV

[15] Psalm 103:13-14, ESV

response to go straight to Jesus when the problems come up. We need to be people who are engaged in a constant conversation and reliance on God to live the life that he desires for us to live and experience. We should constantly be asking God to create in us a first-response reality that takes us straight to Jesus to find help with everything that we face, even the things that we think he has no connection to. He knows all and is the solution to all. His invitation for help is constantly and joyfully given to us. He is able. He wants to help. He knows what we are facing. And he cares, even if the problem is that we run out of our favorite beverage at a wedding. The good carpenter even knows how to make a good 180 bottles of wine.

chapter 03. it can't be that simple.

His mother said to the servants, "Do whatever he tells you."
— John 2:5

"Lather. Rinse. Repeat as needed."

These are the instructions on a bottle of shampoo. Bottle after bottle of shampoo is produced with a label on each bottle giving every person getting ready to wash their hair the same instructions. "Lather. Rinse. Repeat as needed." It seems so simple. But why write them? Because as simple as the directions are to wash one's hair, these are still the directions. It does not matter how simple the task is, each task has directions. And those directions will remain the directions for that task forever.

Life as a Christian is best summed up in these words: *do whatever he tells you.* That is it. But to read those words seems so simple. Almost too simple. We are so used to difficulty that we anticipate it even when it is as simple as washing your hair. We prefer lists that are longer and more grueling because it is then that we are really doing what we are supposed to do (or so we think). But I believe that Jesus wants us to take those lists and bring them all under this one thing: *do whatever he tells you*. It may not always be easy, but it really is that simple.

Remember when Jesus was asked this question by one of the lawyers of his day, "Which commandment is the most important of all?" Jesus answered his question. That was gutsy. We have a hard time nailing down our favorite song, genre of book, or movie, but Jesus answers this question. "What commandment, out of all of the Scriptures, is the greatest commandment of all?" Out of the 613 commandments found in the Law Jesus knew the number one answer because he wrote the book.

He knew the answer because the number one answer was the heartbeat of his being, and this was his chance to make it known. He said, "The most important is: 'Hear, O Israel, the Lord our God, the Lord is one. And you shall love the Lord your God with all your heart and with all your soul and with all your mind and with all your strength."[16] Did you see it? There is one God, and the thing that he wants most from us is simply to love him. Love God with everything that

---

[16] Mark 12:29-30, ESV

we are and in everything that we do.

But then, as if to go above and beyond by connecting the next one with the first, he kept going with number two, "The second is this: 'You shall love your neighbor as yourself.' There is no other commandment greater than these."[17] The lawyer only asked for one commandment – the number one out of all of them. Jesus, like that overachiever kid in your fourth-grade class, gives him the second one free of charge. Love other people. It all comes down to loving God with everything first, and then loving every other person on the planet out of that love that we have for God.

Think of the perspective that heaven had. Here was a man asking Jesus what the most important commandment of God was, all the while not recognizing, along with everyone else there, that it was God who was answering his question. I wonder what the angels were thinking as they watched this conversation unfold.

The conversation between Jesus and this lawyer is brought to light even more from Matthew's perspective of the conversation. Mark leaves out one part that Matthew couldn't shake from his mind. "On these two commandments

---

[17] Mark 12:31, ESV

depend all the Law and the Prophets."[18] So the 613 commandments found in the Law, and every word of the ancient prophets, were summed up in two things: Love God with everything. Love others. The heartbeat of God is not summed up in the long lists of specific commandments. The focus is not to make sure that every one of the 613 commandments is kept with legalistic religious fervor, but to focus on the two commandments that all the other commandments fall under to love God and love others. To obey the two is to obey all of them.

"But it can't be that simple. Every part of the Bible is summed up in two things? There has to be more to it."

The lawyer was stunned and left speechless as Jesus answered his question. "You are right, Teacher. You have truly said that he is one, and there is no other besides him. And to love him with all the heart and with all the understanding and with all the strength, and to love one's neighbor as oneself, is much more than all whole burnt offerings and sacrifices."[19] The simplicity of Jesus' answer was sufficient for the lawyer. The lawyer heard that the profoundly simple heartbeat of

---

[18] Matthew 22:40, ESV

[19] Mark 12:32-33, ESV

God in Jesus' response to his question was as easy as counting to two.

Mary knew this. Mary had told Jesus about the problem, and he asked her, "Woman, what does this have to do with me? My hour has not yet come." It seemed like that should have been the end of the conversation. But there was a reason that God chose Mary to be the mother of Jesus. She was not a random choice, or a "she will work" option. God does not work in those ways. Rather, God handpicked her for a reason. Even after it seemed like Jesus was not interested in helping, she turned to the servants and volunteered her son by saying, "Do whatever he tells you." Mary didn't hear "no" in Jesus' response, she merely heard Jesus ask a question. She knew there was a solution and growing up with Jesus for those thirty years convinced Mary that he could fix this. It was not because he had proven himself through miraculous signs, because he hadn't performed any yet. But there was just something about Jesus, something that maybe he learned from Mary, that there is always a solution.

Can you picture the smirk that came on Jesus' face as he saw that look in his mama's eyes? She didn't answer him, but her next move said more than anything that she could have verbalized. Her next move proclaimed her "faith" in

Jesus, believing that he could take care of it. She went over to the servants and said, "Do whatever he tells you." She volunteered her son to fix the problem, but she recruited the help of others as well. She did not let Jesus off the hook. Rather, she set it up for him to take care of the problem with a group of unsuspecting servants to "assist him." But doesn't this seem a little bold and presumptuous for her to do? No. She was his mom, and moms have a way of volunteering their kids to do things. I think that right just comes with the title "mom." But I wonder if we are invited by Jesus to the same confidence that Mary had in this situation, to "volunteer him" to take care of the impossible situations in our lives.

But here is a question for us today? How can we truly know what Jesus is saying? How can we know what God wants? I think most of us would do what God said if he just made it obvious, like leaving us a text or sending us a letter. Well, that is exactly what he did.

Read his word. Read the Bible.

The longest chapter in all of the Bible is Psalm 119 where the psalmist talks about the goodness of God's commandments, statutes, precepts, and promises. Within the pages of the Bible we see God's work, hear his heart, are taught things that lead us to wisdom, proclaiming the beautiful and redemptive story of the gospel from cover to cover, ultimately leading us to Jesus himself.[20] Reading the Bible may seem like a monotonous exercise, and at times it may seem dry. In reality, however, every time we open the pages of Scripture, no matter how we feel before, during or after our time in it, we are sitting down and hearing from God himself. Of course, we must tune our hearts to listen to what he is saying, while receiving the things that he reveals to us through its pages, but he is always using his word to speak to us.

And then as we spend time in the Scriptures, listening to what he says, we listen and speak to him in prayer. We get honest before him, sharing the things that we are facing and how we want to see him act. We tell him how amazing he is and how we want to see those who do not know Jesus surrender to him. We cry out before him as we feel abandoned and alone. We weep and wail as we wonder if he is going to come through like he says he will. We pray for the physical needs of others and for God to liberate those in

---

[20] "You search the Scriptures because you think that in them you have eternal life; and it is they bear witness about me yet you refuse to come to me that you may have life." — John 5:39-40, ESV

oppression. We even tell him jokes and share with him things that make us laugh. In other words, we talk to him about everything. But while we are invited to be raw and real before God, to say and share anything with him, we must also go before him in prayer to listen. The writer of Ecclesiastes said, "Guard your steps when you go to the house of God. To draw near to listen is better than to offer the sacrifice of fools, for they do not know that they are doing evil. Be not rash with your mouth, nor let your heart be hasty to utter a word before God, for God is in heaven and you are on earth. Therefore let your words be few."[21]

You see, there is a way for us to apply Mary's words to the servants. We can listen to what he says and do it through spending time with Jesus in reading the Bible and being with him in prayer. But also realize that there is something to be said about Mary in this part of the passage that we must also employ. She was able to take the problem straight to Jesus and trust him with the results. She knew about the problem. She knew that there was something wrong. She may have even stood around with the family brainstorming possible solutions. But in the end, she simply went to Jesus, told him

---

[21] Ecclesiastes 5:1-2, ESV (*emphasis* added)

the situation (sounds like prayer), and left it with him.

The apostle Peter, in his first letter, said, "Humble yourselves, therefore, under the mighty hand of God so that at the proper time he may exalt you, casting all your anxieties on him, because he cares for you."[22] Think about the experiences that Peter had with Jesus. Jesus called him to an adventure that would leave him speechless. He called him to a life that included times of bitterness of soul, as he recovered from his three-time denial of Jesus, and joyous celebrations as he watched Jesus perform miracles, including coming back from the dead. He had questions about the kingdom, misunderstanding so much but learning every day more and more from the great Rabbi. And he saw the miraculous. He watched Jesus feed 5,000+ people with a little boy's lunch. He watched Jesus bring Jairus' daughter back from the dead. He saw Jesus restore sight to the blind and hearing to the deaf. He was there when the paralyzed man had to be lowered through the ceiling of his own house by the paralyzed man's friends, but who after meeting Jesus picked up his own mat and walked home unassisted. So, when Peter wrote his letter, he came to this part with total

---

[22] 1 Peter 5:6-7, ESV (*emphasis* added)

confidence in Jesus' ability to get it done—to find the solution even when the solution was utterly impossible. All that he told his readers to do, (now us included) was to humble themselves and give it to Jesus. That's it. We are to humble ourselves and give it to Jesus.

But isn't that the hard part? Handing it off? Giving it to him? It is much more natural for us to just mention it to Jesus, like we would with any of our friends or family members, so that we had someone else who knew what we were going through. Then after we inform him of what is happening, we can go back to running around, aimlessly pretending like we are in control, "fixing" the problem like a little boy with his plastic construction set ready to build a huge skyscraper in downtown New York. The difference with casting it on Jesus is that we give it to the One who has the authority and ability to handle it. The harder part is having to trust him with the results that he wants rather than trying to create our preferred results on our own.

So often it is not an issue of us not believing that Jesus can do something about it. Rather it is about accepting the fact that he actually will do something about it and often not in a way that we are wanting. We know that Jesus can do whatever he wants, but when it is time for him to do whatever he wants in our own lives and situations, that is where we struggle the most.

Remember that this whole walk with Jesus comes back to this one question: who is he? Do you trust him? Do you trust his character? His timing? His reasons? Do you trust his methods to be perfect and right? Do you believe that he is profoundly, perfectly, and always good, and therefore, that all of his ways are good? Do you surrender to his ability to accomplish his will, no matter what that is, so that his desires are accomplished even if yours are not? Are you at a place in your journey with Jesus to release the situation that you are dealing with and then walk away? Are you able to look around at what is going on and volunteer Jesus to do what he does best, to make a solution out of an impossible situation? My challenge to all of us is to simply "volunteer" Jesus. We have a part, but it is not that necessary. We simply abide in him as he abides in us. We learn to completely rely on him, to do what he calls us to do in the process to see his change become a reality in our lives, and then we do whatever he says.

So if we truly believe that he is good, great, and able, let's volunteer Jesus and trust him with what he does best. Let's just make sure that we keep an eye on him. We do not want to miss a thing.

"But is it really that simple?" Maybe over time, it will be. But when we get to that point where it is that simple, we will be all the better for it.

chapter 04. even when it makes no sense.

Now there were six stone jars there for the Jewish rites of purification, each holding twenty or thirty gallons. Jesus said to the servants, "Fill the jars with water." And they filled them up to the brim. —John 2:6-7

Can you feel the tension? The servants were there and heard Jesus get in trouble with mom (or so it may have seemed to them). To them, it sounded like Jesus wasn't interested or able to find a solution to the problem. And I'm sure they could understand why. It was a tough situation. Not life-threatening but tough, nonetheless. So, there they were, standing with Jesus just waiting for him to tell them what to do. Awkward.

Jesus looked over and saw the jars used for ceremonial cleansing during the wedding celebration. Those jars had a specific use already assigned to them, a task of reverence and piety that Jesus just assigned to the mundane. "Using the jars for another purpose would temporarily defile them; Jesus shows more concern for his friend's wedding than for the contemporary ritual."[23] So, Jesus said to the servants, "Do you see those six stone jars over there? Can you go and get those for me?" The servants walked over toward them.

After a couple of trips to get all of the jars, they stood before Jesus, waiting for his next set of instructions to fix the problem. Then they heard the words that would make no sense to any of them. Jesus said, "Now go ahead and fill the jars with water."

"Alright?" one of the servants might have said, with a question in the tone of his voice. "Fill them with water?" he thought. "What is that going to do to fix the problem? That makes no sense." Just to make sure that he heard him correctly, he said to Jesus, "I just want to make sure that I heard you correctly. You want us to fill these six stone jars with water, right? These six stone jars that each hold around 20-30 gallons. Right? You would like for us to get around 180 gallons of water into these six jars because the guests don't have any more wine. Am I hearing you correctly?"

---

[23] Keener, C. S. (1993). *The IVP Bible background commentary: New Testament* (Jn 2:7). Downers Grove, IL: InterVarsity Press.

Jesus looked at them with a straight face, fighting back the grin that began to form as he understood the confusing solution that he had just introduced, and said, "Yep". He understood that the request made no sense to them. He knew that the problem was not that there wasn't enough water for people to drink or to wash their hands. He knew that the problem presented to him by his mom was that there was no more wine. He knew that they would be wondering how this was going to help the situation at all. He knew all of this and still told them to fill the jars, hiding his excitement that very soon their lives would never be the same.

"Okay," the servant said to Jesus.

He went back to his buddies and said, "Let's fill the jars with water." All of them looked at him with confused looks. "I know. It makes no sense. Let's just do what he says." And so, they went to work.

The only way to fill large stone jars in those days was to use smaller buckets. So maybe they carried the water jars to a cart and then moved them to a well. And then one by one the servants would take the bucket, dip it into the well, draw it back up and empty it into the large stone water jar.

Imagine that the bucket held 1 gallon. That means that they would be dropping the bucket into the well, drawing it back up, and emptying it into the large stone jars between 120 and 180 times. Over and over. Just filling the jars.

"Okay. That's enough. It doesn't have to be perfect. He won't care if it's totally full. Come on."

"No. He said to fill them, so we will fill them."

So, they kept filling the jars until "they filled them to the brim." The guests of the wedding had no idea what was going on. They kept going on with the wedding celebration. The parents of the young married couple knew there was a problem. Mary and Jesus knew that there was a problem. But the guests: they were oblivious to it. They continued with the celebration. Jesus didn't make an announcement to the guests so that they knew that the wine was almost gone. He was merely taking care of it. This was all behind the scenes.

177. 178. 179. 180. The servants looked at each other with a small sense of pride and satisfaction that they had finished the task at hand, but with a puzzled spirit as to what exactly they had accomplished. "That's it. We're done. Let's get these back to Jesus." And when they came to Jesus with

the jars filled to the brim, Jesus smiled. Their service pleased him.

Now of course everything that I described already is not taken straight from the pages of the Bible. I took some liberty in trying to paint the scene so that we could connect with how those servants may have felt when Jesus asked them to do the same kinds of things that he asks us to do. "You want me to do what?" "How does that make sense?" Those are just two of the questions that come to our minds when Jesus asks us to do something that is unpredictable, irrational, and uncomfortable. And why would Jesus do this? I think there are a few reasons.

#1. Jesus doesn't do things as we do them.

I have accepted this truth long ago: my first reaction to a situation is most of the time not anywhere close to Jesus' response to that same situation. The reason: I'm not God. He said it this way to Isaiah

> "For my thoughts are not your thoughts,
> neither are your ways my ways, declares
> the LORD. For as high as the heavens are
> above the earth, so are my ways higher
> than your ways and my thoughts than

your thoughts."[24]

It is not that how we think is always wrong and horrible. It is not that we never have good ideas. It is just that compared to the mind of God, why limit ourselves to our own ideas instead of walking forward with him in his limitless perspective? Paul wrote this same idea to the Christians in Rome.

> "Oh, how great are God's riches and wisdom and knowledge! How impossible it is for us to understand his decisions and his ways! For who can know the Lord's thoughts? Who knows enough to give him advice? And who has given him so much that he needs to pay it back? For everything comes from him and exists by his power and is intended for his glory. All glory to him forever! Amen."[25]

---

[24] Isaiah 55:8-9, ESV

[25] Romans 8:33-36, New Living Translation

Our greatest attempt to understand the mind of God is like trying to fit all of the waters on the earth into a teacup. It's just not possible. But would you really want it any other way? Do you really want to be able to completely understand God, and every reason for every decision, clearly understanding his power and ability? All that leaves us with is a deity no bigger nor more impressive than we are. He would not be worthy of worship because he would be no greater than us. And honestly, for some people, this is fine. "How can you worship a God you can't understand" is a question that they will ask, and yet my response is always, "How can you want to worship a God that you can understand?".

The fact that Jesus is beyond me causes me to want to go beyond with him. I find comfort in the fact that I don't understand him because it means that he is able to handle everything that I don't understand. God is limitless so why would I ever expect to be able to understand the limitless from a limited perspective?

#2. Jesus is not intimidated by the things that we are.

There are people and situations that cause our blood pressure to rise because of how intimidated we are by them or by how frustrated they make us. But Jesus is not intimidated by anyone or anything. He is not afraid of people or circumstances. He's never at a loss for ideas or words. His words are perfect, and his ways are surely dependable.

> "To whom will you compare me? Or who is my equal?" says the Holy One. Lift up your eyes and look to the heavens: Who created all these? He who brings out the starry host one by one and calls forth each of them by name. Because of his great power and mighty strength not one of them is missing."[26]

And that is the God that we follow. And since we follow that God, we must accept the fact that he handles situations and deals with people that make us uncomfortable, taking us with him as he goes. The fact that God invites us to follow him and to be used by him to accomplish his will, things that will leave us wondering how it all makes sense and how he made it all come together, leaves me amazed and terrified all at the same time. It makes me wonder what's next, excited about the possibility while at the same time nervous about what God is going to make me do to see it happen. There's no way

---

[26] Isaiah 40:25-26, New International Version

that boredom should ever be a description of the life of any follower of Jesus. Why? The adventure of following Jesus makes boredom an impossibility.

#3. Just to see if we will do it.

Many years back I was having lunch with one of my closest friends. We were chatting about life and family and Jesus. As we were laughing and talking, this young lady, about 20 years of age, walked past us. As she walked past us, this thought came to my mind. "Go over and tell her that she's loved." I didn't say anything to my friend about that random thought. We just kept talking about life. But that thought never stopped. It just kept repeating over and over in my head.

"Go over and tell her that she's loved."

So, I did what I had to do. I started an argument in my head about why I was not going to go over and say those words because I wasn't the right guy for the job. First, I don't make it a habit to go over to young women to tell them that they are loved, especially since I was married. I feel like a single young man should be called to that since it sounds like a cheesy Christian pick-up line. Second, I was almost twice her age at the time (almost is the key term there). Third, I'm not smooth and suave enough to say it so that she wouldn't wonder what type of questionable character was standing in front of her. So, I kept arguing, point by point, seeming to prove why this was such a bad idea.

My buddy and I finished lunch. We refilled our drinks and began to walk outside. He went out first. When I got to the door I couldn't go outside. The thought kept repeating over and over. I stopped in the doorway and my buddy turned around. He looked at me and said, "You have to go do something for Jesus right now don't you?" I said, "Yes. Come with me." He looked at me and said, "Nope." He then walked to his car and drove away. As he walked away, I declared to him, "We are no longer friends." The fact that he didn't turn around made it seem like he was okay with that (we're still friends by the way).

There I was, having to go up to this young lady to tell her that she was loved. So, after about five minutes of standing by the drink station, I began my walk over to her table. As I got closer I noticed that she was eating with one of her friends. So the assignment changed from one young to saying these words in front of two young ladies sitting together having a nice lunch that is about to be completely interrupted and possibly ruined, by this huge bald man.

I was so uncomfortable, but I knew that I had to do it. I finally walked over and put my hands on their lunch table. The problem with that is, at 6 feet 3 inches tall, I looked like this mammoth man standing over them ready to destroy them. Nonetheless, I stood there. They looked up at me as I said, "I'm sorry to interrupt. I don't know if this makes any sense, but I'm supposed to tell you that you're loved." I stood there stiff as a board yet reservedly excited about the miracle that was about to take place. I thought to myself, "There is no way that Jesus would have me do something like this without the miraculous following right behind." This was going to be my moment of glory.

And then it happened. I couldn't believe it.

What happened? NOTHING. That's right. The two young ladies just sat there looking at me straight in the face. No facial expression. No "thank you." No, "I knew it. I want to surrender to Jesus right here right now." Nothing. So, I took my hands off the table, looked at both of them, and said, "Well, see ya later." And that was it.

And as I walked out to my car I asked Jesus, "What was that all about?" And then this thought came to mind: "Just checking." That's right. JUST CHECKING. I'm convinced that Jesus had me go through that just to make sure that I would do it. And I'm convinced that he and all the heavenly host had a nice laugh about the whole situation at my expense.

I know that some of you will encourage me by saying, "You never know what that meant to her." And you are totally right. I have no clue if I dented eternity at that moment for that girl or if I just became the laughable topic of the rest of their lunch. What I do know is that I did not walk to my car with a sense of victory. I didn't walk out high-fiving the other patrons who were sitting in their seats enjoying their lunches, chest-bumping the last one in the line as I walked out to the applause of everyone in that restaurant. I was just trying to get to the car before Jesus had me do something else.

Jesus is not like us, and therefore at times, he will ask us to do things that make no sense, and at times even terrify us. But keep this in mind when he does: he will ask us to do things that make no sense to us so that he is the one that is noticed when it is all over. And when it is all over, I believe we will stand amazed at how he brought it all together. The hardest part about following through with Jesus' "irresponsible and unpredictable" requests is being faithful—completely faithful. When the task is something that gets other people's attention and leaves us looking incredible, the task seems a lot easier to follow through with. But when the task is mundane and unnoticed or makes no sense to us in bringing about any positive outcome, that's when faithfulness takes a whole lot more effort.

The servants who filled the jars at the command of Jesus were faithful in the task assigned to them. They filled the jars—to the brim. They may not have understood why they were filling jars, but they filled them, nonetheless. Because of their faithfulness, they are our examples of what we are called to do when Jesus commands us to do what seems irrational. We take the role of servants who are assigned tasks by Jesus to do what he says as situations arise and as he sees fit. We are not the guests of honor or the focus of everyone's attention. Rather, we are the servants who are working behind the scenes.

But along with Jesus asking us to do things that make no sense to us, he will also call us to be faithful to the tasks that no one will ever know that we did. He will call us to do the following types of things:

- Love our spouses.
- Love our kids.
- Teach our kids how to ride a bike.
- Love our family and friends.
- Serve the poor.
- Work in the youth group.
- Work in the nursery.
- Reach out to our neighbors.
- Mow our neighbor's lawn.
- Fix our neighbor's cars.
- Write a letter or send a text of encouragement to someone.
- Let someone move over in front of us in traffic.
- Pray for the person in the next booth.
- Bring in our neighbor's trashcans without them knowing.
- Pay for the meal of the person behind us in the drive-thru.
- Honor our parents.

- Lovingly confront a fellow Christian if they are living in sin.
- Run our businesses above reproach, striving to create an environment in the workplace that people want to be part of and where Jesus is honored.
- Pray with a stranger.
- Offer our tithe at the church where we are involved in serving.
- Help a neighbor fix a broken sprinkler head.
- Teach our students.
- Cry with the broken.
- Rejoice with those who rejoice.
- Listen to a person's fears and struggles.
- Tell someone that they are loved.
- Tell someone about Jesus and the beauty of the gospel message.
- Go and make disciples who make disciple-makers.

And the list goes on and on. These things will not bring out any camera crews. No one will stop us and ask for our autographs. No one will write books or make movies based on our obedience to the ordinary and mundane things assigned to us every day. No one will pull out their smartphones to take a picture to post to social media with the hashtag #lookatthisdiscipleofJesus.

In fact, most of the things that we do for Jesus will never be noticed by anyone but Jesus. But does it matter? Isn't the sole reason for our obeying Jesus simply to obey Jesus? Shouldn't the whole reason that we do anything be for the applause of heaven and the standing ovation of Christ? The truth is this: we are called to be faithful in the mundane. Not every prompting of the Holy Spirit will be to jump on a plane and go halfway around the world to share our faith, but rather to just go across the street to share Jesus with our neighbor. He can and does call people to travel all over the world – wherever he wants. I will never limit his calling. But I am confident that every Christian is called to a mission (to go and make disciples) and mission field, and that mission field is usually their zip code. That calling doesn't seem as impressive as other callings, but we need to remember that the impressiveness of the call is connected to the one who called us, not the destination that we are called to.

No matter where we are or what we do, or who our neighbors are, Jesus has called us to simple faithfulness in the mundane, even when it makes no sense and when no one notices or cares about what we are doing. We do because we love Jesus and because Jesus is worth it. How will you respond? How will I? Will we fill the jars—even to the brim?

chapter 05. do it.

And he said to them, "Now draw some out and take it to the master of the feast." So they took it. When the master of the feast tasted the water now become wine, and did not know where it came from (though the servants who had drawn the water knew), the master of the feast called the bridegroom and said to him, "Everyone serves the good wine first, and when people have drunk freely, then the poor wine. But you have kept the good wine until now." — John 2:8-10

The jars were filled with water. The servants did exactly what Mary told them to do: they simply did what Jesus said. They spent however long it took them to fill 180 gallons worth of water to "fix" the problem of no more wine. The job was finished. And just when they were about to turn around to get back to other tasks, Jesus said something like this: "Do me a favor. Take a cup and dip it into the jar and then take that cup over to the master of the feast."

"You have got to be kidding me."

Nothing happened. Nothing changed. All that Jesus did was ask them to fill a cup up with water. The problem was still present, and the situation had not changed at all. But since they had already spent so much time doing what he said, what's one more thing to do? But notice that one person did not take it over the master of ceremonies. Rather, *they* took it. All the servants who helped fill the jars up with water went together to take one cup over to the master of the feast. Why? Why would they all go? It's just a cup. It's not like it's heavy or burdensome. Why would they all have to go over together to take this cup to the master of the feast?

I have two opinions on this. One, because no one was going to look like a fool alone. If they all started together, they were all going to go down together in a blaze of glory. So, they all went with the cup in hand to present the "solution" to the master of the feast. A cup of water. The problem of no more wine was about to be fixed by the servants holding a cup of water (note the sarcasm). And the second is that maybe they all had this feeling that something incredible was about to happen. The passage doesn't tell us. In either case, they all went.

The master of the feast took a sip. Then another. He then looked at the servants with a look in his eye. He called the bridegroom over. As the bridegroom made his way over to him, what were the servants thinking? At that moment I would be trying with everything in me to come up with some clever response to their question, "Why would you bring us water?" I would just be standing there, my mind whirling with the number of unacceptable excuses as to why I stood there with a cup of water.

But the master of the feast asked, "Why have you saved the best wine for the end of the wedding celebration instead of serving it first? No one does it this way." Can you imagine the jaws of each of those servants dropping to the floor with this look of awed confusion on their faces? Can you imagine the conversation that would begin right after hearing the master's comments to the bridegroom? "What just happened?" None of them would be able to answer that question. All that they did was fill the jars with water. After they had done that, they filled a cup up with water and handed it to the master of the feast. But the miracle of Christ happened somewhere between them drawing the water from the jar and the master of the feast tasting the water turned to wine. There was no way to explain what had just happened without jumping to a conclusion of magic trick or miracle. But from the Bible's perspective, it was a miracle — the water became wine. The molecular structure in that cup changed from water into the best wine ever tasted.

Problem solved? Yes. But so much more than that happened that day.

Again, the crowd had no clue what was going on. The crowd was simply celebrating the new marriage of their friends. But to the servants? They just witnessed the very first miracle of Jesus, God-incarnate. They had the front-row seat to the miraculous because they were simply willing to obey Jesus in the mundane. That which seemed so ordinary, yet out of place in fixing the problem, became the first recorded miracle of the Messiah because some servants did what he said. We don't know their names. We don't know anything about them except this: they were used by the Messiah to accomplish the miraculous because of their willingness to be faithful in the mundane.

We are so quick to request from God to experience the miraculous. We want to be able to share with others *that* thing that we were able to see first-hand. We want those stories that everyone walks away from in awe, wondering why we were so lucky to get to see it happen, better yet, to be part of it. But are we as quick to be faithful to obey Jesus, even when he instructs us to do something that is not impressive and will go completely unnoticed?

One day after a worship gathering I was standing up front waiting for people to come up who wanted me to pray with them. After waiting a while, this young couple came up. I had seen them before but hadn't officially met them yet. After they introduced themselves to me, I asked, "How can I pray for you?" She began to share with me, with tears streaming down her cheeks, how she had had shoulder pain for the past 10 years. What made this even harder on her was that she was a physical therapy Ph.D. student at USC. I asked her, "Have you asked someone if this shoulder problem will affect your ability to do what you're going to school for?" She said, "Yes." And with even more tears coming down she explained that she had been told that she wouldn't be able to practice physical therapy for long because of the pain she was experiencing.

So right there, we prayed. As I began to pray, the account of Jesus healing the woman with the twelve-year flow of blood came to my mind. Then, the account of Jesus healing the leper came to mind, especially his request of Jesus. His request was simply this: "Lord, if you will, you can make me clean."[27] That was it. No begging. Not even a request. He simply stated his faith in Christ's ability and left the decision up to him. So that's exactly how I started to pray. I prayed, "Jesus if you want to, you can completely heal Michelle's shoulder. We know that. So, we leave it up to you." I finished praying. We all looked at each other and then I asked, "How's your shoulder?" I asked because I have a conviction that if you pray for someone's healing you ask them right after you pray if they were healed. She said, "I think it feels better," but she wasn't quite sure. And in all honesty, I was skeptical that what she felt was in her mind. I then told her, "Ok. Well, here's the deal. You have to email me tomorrow if it's feeling better. Deal?" She agreed.

The next day I received a long email from her. Long emails can be really good or they can be really bad. She started by saying, "Today I went swimming and my shoulder felt the best that it has felt in ten years." I stopped after reading that and SCREAMED!!! I couldn't believe what I was reading. She had written more but I had to stop right there

---

[27] Matthew 8:2, ESV

and thank Jesus. After that, I replied to her email with so much joy and excitement.

A couple of days later I emailed her again. I wanted to see how she was doing; if her shoulder was still feeling good. She replied within an hour. Here's what she said:

I have had no constant shoulder pain with only minimal twinges when I put it in compromising positions. This is the best I have ever felt! I normally have difficulty sleeping through the night because rolling on my shoulder would wake me up. I have slept through the night every night since Sunday.

The next day I saw her. I asked how she was feeling, and she shared some incredible news. She shared how she had gone to her physical therapy appointment earlier that day. As the therapist was moving her shoulder around like normal, he noticed something. He looked at her and said something like, "It's like your shoulder was never hurt." When she told me that I almost teared up because I thought about the fact that I got to be in the front-row seat of watching Jesus do the miraculous. She was completely and totally healed by Jesus. It had nothing to do with the words that I prayed. It had nothing to do with the fact that I'm a pastor. Rather, it had everything to do with the fact that she came forward in faith, I prayed a simple faith-driven prayer, and Jesus decided to heal her. And I had the amazing opportunity to witness it all. No one stayed to take pictures. No one interviewed me after I said, "Amen." I simply prayed and the miraculous happened right in front of our eyes.

But here's the thing about witnessing the miraculous: it almost always comes at the expense of watching someone hurt or suffer. Some will say, "I look up in the skies and see God's miraculous. The sunrise is an everyday reminder of God's miracles in my life." And I would completely and unapologetically agree with them. Those sights in the heavens leave me speechless and are the result of Jesus holding all things together (Colossians 1:17). There's almost nothing else on the planet that calms my heart more than one of those sunrises or sunsets that look like they were painted by Rembrandt. But what about the miracles that we need God to do to specifically change and affect a specific person in a specific situation?

Miracles are rarely needed when things are great. Instead, miracles are requested of God when there is nothing else that we can do. When there are no other options, we pray and plead for God to intervene with the miraculous. The problem becomes too big. The situation is beyond bearable. The urgency of the situation causes despair and hopelessness. Discouragement sets in. It is even possible for us to look at God and blame him for letting that thing happen or get angry with him because he didn't change it when we know that he could.

The truth is that the miraculous of God is most often ushered in by the crises of life. We all want "the story" that we can tell others, of how God intervened with a miracle, but when the problem arises, the first thing that we do is to ask, and sometimes demand, him to take it away. We want the miracle but want to avoid the pathway by which God decides to introduce it to us. We do whatever it takes to set the problem aside. And when things don't change, we can get bitter.

Here's what I've noticed about living in bitterness: I can't see miracles when my vision is clouded by my bitterness. I can't see God's work in and around my situations when all that I'm doing is blaming him for what he isn't doing. As we looked at earlier in this book, God does what he wants in the way that he wants to do it. In my imagination, I picture God responding to my situations according to how I would respond to them. But the thing with God is this: when all we see are two options, he sees a myriad of responses because he is not limited by the practical or confined by what makes sense. The miraculous almost never makes sense, and that is the playground that God likes to play in the most.

The servants in the passage that we have been looking at saw the miraculous work of Jesus because of a crisis that the family was facing. It is easy for us to look at their situation and say, "No more wine? Come on. Grow up. That's not even a real problem." And then explain how our problems are worse than theirs. But think about it: to an infinite, sovereign, and all-powerful God, should we ever be completely overcome by the crises that we face? This is not my attempt to trivialize the brokenness that humanity experiences but rather to remind us of the truth that God is able to do more. And since he truly is able, shouldn't that affect how we approach him and how we perceive the unwelcomed situations that enter our lives?

We have problems. Jesus told us that we would have trouble in this world. But the fact that we have him to walk through life with should change our perspectives greatly. This is not the guilt-them-to-stop-worrying part of the book, but rather a reminder to all of us, myself especially, that I am invited to live a life of no worry because the God who measures the universe with the span of his hand knows exactly how to deal with each situation that comes my way. He has a plan in all of it, and that plan will often affect so many other people than just me.

When we face trouble, I think we should do whatever we can to take care of the situation. When we see or read about the broken and hurting around the world, those who are experiencing social injustice or extreme poverty and hunger, we should step forward as part of God's agents of change, involved in his solution of caring for his creation. The truth is that we live in a broken world, broken by a man and a wife who ultimately fell into the temptation of wanting to be like God, and we see the after-effects of that decision. And sin has been passed down to every person who has ever lived, including us.

As we look at suffering, we try to make sense of it all. If God is so sovereign, then why does he let this stuff happen? Or if it's all based on our ability to choose and God is simply reacting to situations as we are, then, again, why doesn't he react quicker? It becomes overwhelming to us, leaving us with more questions because our finite minds cannot understand the truth in the answer. But when nothing seems to be working, and we have prayed through it and brought it to God, maybe the best thing that we can do is sit back, take a breath, relax, and wait to see what he does with it and if he wants us as part of his solution. And as we do let's pay attention to what it is that he is doing in us through the crisis.

If Jesus can turn water into wine in the amount of time it takes to go from one side of a room to another, try to imagine what he has in mind for your situation. And then think about what your face will look like when you have the front-row seat to his miraculous.

chapter 06. the importance of the firsts.

This, the first of his signs, Jesus did at Cana in Galilee... — John 2:11

Firsts are always important. Firsts are what cause us to open the camera app on our smartphones to capture important moments. Firsts are what cause us to video chat with family and friends so that they can join in with the celebration. Firsts are those events that cause us to post too many hashtags on social media for no apparent reason except that we want to make the moment live on. Firsts are those events that cause us to travel across the country to be part of the party. I'm guessing that somewhere someone has pictures of many of your firsts.

- Your first smile
- Your first laugh
- Your first time rolling over, standing up, crawling, walking, etc.

- Your first day of kindergarten (and the first day of every grade thereafter)
- First class play
- First baseball game
- First dance recital
- First karate tournament
- Your first time riding a bike
- Losing your first tooth
- Your first school dance
- Your first date
- Your first day of college

And then you begin your list of firsts for yours and others, recording every self-defined momentous occasion, "Self-defined" because what is monumental to you is not monumental to the majority of the population on planet earth.

Firsts are important because of what they are... firsts. And in this passage, we see Jesus perform his FIRST miracle. This is what kicked off his ministry. Turning water into wine. Not raising someone from the dead. Not driving a demon out of a little boy. Not giving sight to the blind or hearing to the deaf. Not giving the paralytic the gift of movement, the ability to pick up his mat and walk out on his own in front of everyone in attendance. Not defying the laws of nature by taking a stroll on top of the Sea of Galilee instead of walking around it. Not calming wind and water, proving his authority over nature. Rather, Jesus inconspicuously turned water into wine at a wedding without an audience, except for a handful of servants who had to fill the jars so that the miraculous would happen and a few disciples who were with him in attendance. That's it. It doesn't seem like the type of miracle to launch on, the kind of miracle that causes the masses to stop and notice. It seems kind of small compared to everything that Jesus would do after that.

Matthew gives us a glimpse of Jesus's other miracles:

And he went throughout all Galilee, teaching in their synagogues and proclaiming the gospel of the kingdom and healing every disease and every affliction among the people. So his fame spread throughout all Syria, and they brought him all the sick, those afflicted with various diseases and pains, those oppressed by demons, epileptics, and paralytics, and he healed them. And great crowds followed him from Galilee and the

Decapolis, and from Jerusalem and Judea,
and from beyond the Jordan."[28]

Matthew tells us that Jesus called his first disciples while they were fishing , which was their normal routine Then he goes on to explain the first things that they witnessed as his disciples. That means that somewhere between his calling them and performing the miracles in Matthew 4, Jesus took them to a wedding. And it was at this wedding where Jesus showed his immense and incredible power by... turning water into wine. Why was this his first? Was it just because Mary asked him to fix the problem of no more wine at the wedding? Did she interrupt his plans, kind of forcing his hand to do anything just to help? Or was there something else to it?

If we are honest, we would admit that it is so easy for us to grade God when it comes to him performing the miraculous. We turn into Olympic gymnastics judges, holding the miraculous under the microscope of our preferences, comfort levels, or expectations, looking for any small thing to cause him to lose points. If the miracle doesn't hold up to our

---

[28] Matthew 4:23-25, ESV

level of scrutiny, then it wasn't as impressive as most of his other ones have been. Or if it can be explained away, then the miracle never happened.

For example: have you ever had someone ask you to pray for them because of a scary diagnosis they received from a doctor, resulting in the doctor wanting to run more tests? I'm sure you have just as I have. Maybe you're the person who asked for prayer because you were the one having to face the possibility of terrible news becoming a reality. So, we pray. We pray hard. We hold nothing back, believing that God can do anything. We pray the type of prayer where we expect to levitate during it because of how much faith is flowing through our blood vessels.

The person goes through the extra tests and then waits for the results, and if you've had to wait for results you know the agony that comes with that. We hang out with them and try to encourage them, texting Bible verses that remind them of the fact that God is in control and can handle anything. We find that perfect quote in a specific book that we've been reading that reminds them of God's love for them and his ability to change the normal into something that we would call a miracle. We share that quote, blog, or line from a song as we wait for the results. We take them to dinner and invite them to baseball games to just help keep their minds off that which they are trying desperately to not think about.

Then we get the phone call: "IT CAME BACK CLEAR!!!" All is well. And our first reaction is, "Thank God that it wasn't what the doctor thought it was." But what if the doctor was right in the first place and God actually healed your friend? What if God has done more in the realm of the miraculous than we could ever imagine and all the while we've given credit to coincidence, false test findings, common means, or modern medicine?

And what about you being used in your friend's life to encourage them through the whole situation? "What? I was just being a good friend. They needed encouragement and I love them so much." But Paul is the one who reminds us, "Blessed be the God and Father of our Lord Jesus Christ, the Father of mercies and God of all comfort, who comforts us in all our affliction, so that we may be able to comfort those who are in any affliction, with the comfort with which we ourselves are comforted by God."[29] The fact that we have been comforted by each other during times of trouble is a miraculous event, for the truth is that God miraculously intervenes with comfort by using those of us whom he has comforted before. As we are comforted by God, we are used by God to comfort others. But is this impressive enough for us? Would we actually consider it a miracle? For the most part no, resulting in us never recognizing the miracle for what it is. George Bernard Shaw once said, "If we could see the miracle of a single flower clearly, our whole life would change." And yet a flower has become ordinary. Beautiful? Yes. But still ordinary.

And what about when a person surrenders to Christ? She is with you and the conversation moves from the weather and work updates to the meaning of life and Jesus. The change of topic is so drastic that it takes you off-guard, but you have been praying and waiting for this opportunity. And the moment arrives. You share with her everything about Jesus and his gospel, leaving room in your explanation for the many questions that flood her mind. You lovingly and

---

[29] 2 Corinthians 1:3-4, ESV

patiently answer each question the best that you can, second-guessing yourself and your answers during the whole conversation. You feel like you're in a wrestling match with yourself, convinced that what you are trying to say is nothing close to what Jesus wants you to share. And then it happens: she says, "I want Jesus."

Your jaw drops. You are filled with the type of excitement that a six-year-old experiences when his parents surprise him with a puppy. You pray together and then go your separate ways. You tell a few friends about it and they share in your excitement. You may even throw out a post on social media so that Christians around the world can rejoice in the good news. Why are we so excited about this? Because we were able to witness and be part of seeing the most powerful miracle on the planet happen: you just saw your friend pass from being dead to being alive—the most impressive miracle of all—right in front of your eyes.

We prefer the "impressive" miracles such as God splitting the Red Sea or Jesus walking on water. The other ones? The ones that look "normal" seem "too normal" compared to what Hollywood can do with special effects in any movie today. We forget that God's idea of the miraculous is anything that he does to alter the "normal" to accomplish his purposes. And anytime God steps in, we are in the presence of the divine and in the perfect position to witness the miraculous.

Jesus didn't touch the water. He didn't fill the cup up for the servants. Rather, he saw the problem, invited the servants to be part of the solution, and "left it alone." He couldn't be accused of a magic trick or playing a prank. And even if he did "spike" that first cup, he couldn't have spiked the rest of the 180 gallons of water, turning it into the best wine the master of ceremonies had ever tasted. But somehow it changed. Somehow that water became wine. The miraculous happened and everything changed that day.

I know that some people who read this chapter will say, "Are you really going to look for the miraculous in so many things?" To this, I will say, ABSOLUTELY! I prefer to have a faith in the impressive and awe-inspiring Jesus that is described in the Bible instead of the impotent and less impressive one that so many people have settled on today. I prefer to let God be God and for my faith to grow and build up a passion in me, rather than a boring belief system that leaves me wondering if Jesus can really do anything. I guess I prefer to see the miraculous of God in the mundane things of life so that I am seeing God constantly at work, as I believe him to be. I don't want to force the miraculous, but rather I want to recognize God's miraculous.

John wrote at the end of his gospel, "Now Jesus did many other signs in the presence of the disciples, which are not written in this book; but these are written so that you may believe that Jesus is the Christ, the Son of God and that by believing you may have life in his name."[30] I wonder what those things were. I wonder what they are today. So much of my normal day will feel normal. So will yours. I probably won't experience a burning bush today. I probably won't walk across the Jordan river on the dry ground during flood season because God decided to stop the water flow. I bet if I try to walk on the top of a deep puddle today, I will probably find myself at the bottom of it quickly. In fact, most of my life will probably be spent being faithful in mundane tasks that no one will take notice of. But I want to make sure that I am being faithful in the mundane things that God wants me to do because he is worthy of my obedience and I love him so

---

[30] John 20:30-31, ESV

much. But also it's so that I'm in the perfect place to see his miraculous when he decides to do it. I want to live with a child-like expectancy of, "Are you gonna do something today, Jesus?" And if he decides to do his work without really making it known in some unbelievable way, that's fine. Hopefully tomorrow. But if he does, I'll be ready.

Remember: the servants weren't expecting to see a miracle that day. They were merely doing their job. But Jesus interrupted their "mundane" tasks to show up and show off for them.

As I've stated before: my job is to be faithful in the mundane and leave the miraculous to Jesus. The when and where and how of the miraculous is his job. My job? Celebrate when it happens. I would much rather be like the servants who were able to witness and celebrate because the miraculous happened in their midst than to be like the wedding guests who were oblivious to the fact that the divine touched the ordinary that day, changing everything.

As I've looked at this passage over and over, I've been left in awe of Jesus' first miracle. And I bet that Mary was blown away by what Jesus did that day. I bet that Mary took a mental picture of Jesus' first miracle, the miracle that changed everything. Why? Because moms can't help but remember their kids' firsts because their firsts are always impressive. And Jesus' first was but a drop in the ocean of what he had already actually done (being that he was the one who actually created the ocean), and what he was going to do. And that miracle of turning water into wine was actually pointing us to the greatest sacrifice that bring about the miracle of Christ's resurrection from the dead. It really all comes down to this one thing: perspective. Do you have the right perspective? Do I? Oh God, give us your perspective so that might see the amazing thing that you are actually up to.

chapter 07. unexpected results.

...and manifested his glory. And his disciples believed in him. —
John 2:11

If we are honest with ourselves, most of us want to live a life of significance. The majority of us want to know that our being here on this planet was for a reason, that we lived in such a way that others will show up to our funerals with at least a few nice things to say because we left an impact on them. It just seems like it is woven into the fabric of our being to matter. Of course, you may be reading this, completely disagreeing with me because you don't have a purpose and aren't really looking to find it. You're just "enjoying life," living for every pleasure that comes your way. And if that's you, can I, very lovingly but directly, ask you a question: how is that working out for you? How is it working out for you to just wake up to live a day, to experience the same things, and go back to bed at the end of it, just to repeat it again tomorrow?

My guess, and this is only a guess, of course, is that it leaves you feeling empty—as if there is something missing.

There is only so much *disconnected* monotony that we can take without being led down a road of discouragement and boredom. If there's no purpose to the monotonous, then why even do it? Honestly, why really do anything? But that is where Jesus changes everything. He is the only one who can take the disconnected monotony and connect it to his miraculous plan, giving us a divine purpose that leaves us amazed and fulfilled as we simply walk with him. I'm not saying that every day is a mountain-top experience that leaves us breathless. However, I am saying that Jesus gives us a reason for journeying in the first place, whether it's across the mountain peaks that leave us amazed because of the view or through the valleys that leave us broken and hurting, wondering if we are going to be able to make it to the next mountaintop while learning to rely on him (2 Corinthians 1:9). But even between those two places in the journey, there's the plateau. There will be many miles traveled across the plains and plateaus, taking one step after another, following Jesus who walks through every ordinary step with us—leading us down a road that is oftentimes... ordinary.

As we've walked together through this book so far, we go back to the servants who simply did what Jesus said. They filled some jars with water to fix the problem of no more wine. They filled them to the brim. Bucket full of water after bucket full of water, transferring each bucket into the large jars until each jar was filled. They were doing "their job." But their simple obedience accomplished two life and time-changing things.

1. JESUS MANIFESTED HIS GLORY.

The psalmist said it this way: "Not to us, O LORD, not to us, but to your name give *glory*, for the sake of your steadfast love and your faithfulness."[31] The apostle Paul summed it up this way when he wrote one of his letters to the community of believers in the city of Corinth: "For God, who said, 'Let light shine out of darkness,' has shone in our hearts to give the light of the knowledge of the *glory* of God in the face of Jesus Christ."[32] The apostle John wrote about what was revealed to him on the Isle of Patmos, as he watched four living creatures that looked like something out of the "Lord of the Rings" trilogy giving glory and honor and

---

[31] Psalm 115:1, ESV

[32] 1 Corinthians 4:6, ESV

thanks to Jesus, saying, "Holy, holy, holy is the Lord God Almighty, who was and is and is to come!"[33] But with this incredible declaration of praise and worship and adoration, the twenty-four elders responded by falling down before Jesus, throwing their crowns before the throne. And in one voice they said, "Worthy are you, our Lord and God, to receive *glory* and honor and power, for you created all things, and by your will they existed and were created."[34]

In Russell Moore's book, "Tempted and Tried," he attempts to describe the glory of God this way. I say "attempted" not because it was a lousy attempt, but because it is impossible to fully describe God's glory. But here is what he says:

> *Glory* in biblical thought is the unapproachable, uncreated light that surrounds the triune God. Glory is also the fame and renown and acclaim of God. But glory also includes a theatrical component. It is the public display of God's

---

[33] Revelation 4:8, ESV

[34] Revelation 4:11, ESV

goodness, truth, and beauty, and thus his praiseworthiness. One theologian defines God's glory as, in part, God's right to prove, declare, and "almost as it were to make himself conspicuous and everywhere apparent as the One he is." Another notes that what it means for God to be glorified is that "each member of the Trinity speaks and acts in such a way as to *enhance the reputations* of the other two, to bring praise and honor to the other persons."[35]

Did you see that last description? The idea that each member of the Trinity—Father, Son, and Holy Spirit—speaks and acts in such a way as to *enhance the reputations of the other two* is mind-blowing. The beautiful relationship between the members of the Trinity is our example of how to mutually submit to each other, not striving to be first and the

---

[35] Moore, Russell, *Tempted and Tried: Temptation and the Triumph of Christ*. Crossway; Wheaton, Illinois, pg. 116.

only one noticed, but rather truly and humbly placing others above ourselves. The Father, Son, and Holy Spirit are constantly trying to enhance the reputation of the other, giving each other the glory that is due all of them.

And I believe that is the key to our understanding of how these servants manifested Christ's glory. It's not that they showed Jesus in the fullness of his glory, for that was impossible for them to do. Rather, because of their willingness to be faithful in the mundane, right where Jesus had called them to be, they enhanced the reputation of this Jewish carpenter who could do the miraculous. The servants remained nameless while Jesus' reputation spread. And that's exactly what it's supposed to be like for us today.

2. HIS DISCIPLES BELIEVED IN HIM.

The miraculous hadn't happened yet in front of his disciples. As far as they knew Jesus merely invited them to go to a wedding with him. Little did they know that they were about to see the first miracle performed by God incarnate. God had done the miraculous in the past. They had heard the stories before in their little Sunday school classes and around the kitchen table. But this wasn't like those times. Why? Because God did those things while remaining concealed. The people couldn't see him while he performed the miracles. They just knew that it was him because he made it that obvious.

The disciples stood there and listened to Jesus tell the servants what to do. Then they waited. I can guarantee that they weren't expecting a miracle. Rather, I think maybe they were relieved that Jesus didn't ask them to help. And I wonder if they felt for the servants when they came back in, exhausted, after filling the jars up with 180 gallons of water. BUT everything changed after that.

Imagine the thoughts that rushed through their minds when they saw the reaction of the master of the ceremonies. Imagine the confusion and amazement that saturated their souls as they watched the expressions of the servants change from exhaustion to passionate celebration and childlike wonder. Imagine the thoughts that rushed through their minds when they heard the servants screaming, "IT'S WINE!!!" And imagine the faith that wrapped their souls as they looked at the grin on the face of Jesus. The disciples believed and everything changed, all because some servants filled up some jars. Oswald Chambers summarizes this idea behind the mundane miracles of God:

> "We look for visions from heaven, for earthquakes and thunders of God's power (the fact that we are dejected proves that we do), and we never dream that all the time God is in the commonplace things and people around us. If we will do the duty that lies nearest, we shall see Him. One of the most amazing revelations of God comes when we learn that it is in the commonplace things that the Deity of Jesus Christ is realized."

Some guys filled some jars. Disciples believed in Jesus. Those disciples of Jesus then began a three-year journey, walking in the footsteps of their Rabbi. They watched him perform miracles. They heard him preach the truth about the kingdom of God. They watched him love the unloved and forgotten. They watched him play with the children. They watched him die on a cross. They met him resurrected from the dead. They went out and proclaimed the gospel all over the world, making disciples of all nations. And all of this because some guys filled some jars. That's the simplicity behind what they did. And that's really all that we are called to do. It really is simple: just do whatever Jesus says, even if all that he tells us to do is fill some jars.